Praise for *Landlock X*

"Nothing about hunger is passive," writes Sarah Audsley in this deft debut. That a poet as versed in detail and image would choose to write within the pastoral tradition is not surprising. What surprises, however, is the way Audsley uses the pastoral as a vehicle to express many griefs: loss of a mother; loss of a country; loss of a culture; and even loss of a way of life. Despite an abundance of grief, *Landlock X* stands not as simple elegy but as a triumph of the self. This is a powerful collection.

    — C. Dale Young, author of *Prometeo*

In this stunning debut collection, Sarah Audsley shapes a narrative out of an incomplete history and creates a living artifact, forging a history for herself and her family. "I am the *X* / inside a body," she writes, but the poems offer no easy solutions. In her explorations of the various forces that create and define a self, these poems remind us how history is never simply individual, but communal. *Landlock X* is a testament to the act of writing as an act of love.

    — Christine Kitano, author of *Sky Country*

In *Landlock X*, Sarah Audsley makes of lyric an intimate journey toward an impossible beginning. Toward what it means to belong, to see (and be seen), to insist on connection—fraught and forged—in and through profound severance. I am so moved by how, where reclamation may not be an option, Audsley intervenes with imagination, intellectual and emotional breadth, and courage, to "choose [her] own extent." This work simultaneously indicts and consoles; it roams colors, oceans, flowers, the black holes of lineage and nation(s), and stands its ground. "Almost drowning is touching creation," writes the poet, and I am compelled to reconsider the solidities I take for granted. To be alive.

    — Cynthia Dewi Oka, author of *Fire Is Not a Country*

Sarah Audsley's *Landlock X* is a book I wish I had been able to read years ago. With language sharp and lucid as a cut gem, these poems spin the yellows of hay and light into gold and pursue difficult questions and answers without flinching. Audsley's precise excavations of personal history, through archival images and such forms as the sijo and haibun, examine what facts remain after erasure and translation have scraped away at memory. In this brilliant field of poems, each moon is a face or a flipped rabbit, the distances between "I" and "you" and "*X*" are measurable, and home becomes strange as strangers become home. This book calls across time and oceans and listens for your response. "[Y]ou, dear adoptee, are not alone. / I am lonely, too."

    — Marci Calabretta Cancio-Bello, author of *The Hour of the Ox*

LANDLOCK X

Library of Congress Cataloging-in-Publication Data

Names: Audsley, Sarah, author.
Title: Landlock X : poems / Sarah Audsley.
Description: First edition. | Huntsville : TRP: The University Press of
    SHSU, [2023]
Identifiers: LCCN 2022039060 (print) | LCCN 2022039061 (ebook) | ISBN
    9781680033052 (paperback) | ISBN 9781680033069 (ebook)
Subjects: LCSH: Adopted children--Vermont--Poetry. | Korean American
    children--Vermont--Ethnic identity--Poetry. | Birthparents--Poetry. |
    Country life--Vermont--Poetry. | Nature--Poetry. | Imaginary
    letters--Poetry. | LCGFT: Epistolary poetry. | Experimental poetry.
Classification: LCC PS3601.U343 L36 2023 (print) | LCC PS3601.U343
    (ebook) | DDC 811/.6--dc23/eng/20220819
LC record available at https://lccn.loc.gov/2022039060
LC ebook record available at https://lccn.loc.gov/2022039061

Cover design by Bradley Alan Ivey
Cover Image: Nancy Y. Kim, *how a yellow hollow*, 2021,
Paper Pulp, Silicone, Acrylic Paint, 25.5 x 22.5cm / 10 x 8.9 in.
Photo Credit: Marco Ravenna

Printed and bound in the United States of America

Published by TRP: The University Press of SHSU
Huntsville, Texas 77341
texasreviewpress.org

LANDLOCK X

Poems
Sarah Audsley

TRP: The University Press of SHSU
Huntsville, Texas

TABLE OF CONTENTS

III. PORTAL

[untranslated]

안녕하세요 이소현 선생님 바쁘신 업무에도

너의옷 부탁을 들어주시고 이렇게 연락까지

전해주셔서 여러가지로 감사드립니다

※ 과은맞을 어디서부터 어떻게 외모말을 먼저

시와할지 모르겠지만 막상 글을 쓸려니까

손이떨려서 긴장도 되고 사실 그만도 되는구나

하더만 보고 싶었다 30년동안 항상 마음에 두고

생각했다 자식버린 부모가 무슨할말이 있겠지만

그래서 항상 생각하고 보고싶고 궁금했다

사실 지영이를 입양보낸것은 지영이가 태어난지

한달만에 엄마가 갑자기 세상을 떠나

손 쓸새도 없이 세곁을 떠나버린거야

그래도 나는 지영이를 우리를넘어나와 살면서

키우려고 했지만 농사를 짓다보니 지영이를

거사할 시간이 없고 그리고 여건이 따라주질

않아서 생각끝에 입양하기로 마음먹고

오천소에 연락해서 좋은부모 만나게 해달라며

너를 보낸것이다 그러니 나를 용서해라

나를 보낸지 30년이 지난 지금은 좋은부모 만나

예쁘게 잘컸는지 궁금하고 결혼한 나이가 되었는데

결혼은 했는지 궁금하고 보고 싶구나

부모라고 자식라고 책임못지고 입양보낸 나를 용서해라

SUNG WON

정말 미안하고 또 미안하다

그리고 지영이를 입양보내고 몇년후 지금 애들엄마
를 만나서 결혼하고 두아배 낳아서 키우고
공장 다니면서 살다가

15년 3년은 떠나 지금은 전라북도 정읍시에서
작은 아파트에서 살다가

11년전 가까운 시골에 조그마한 땅을 사서
농사를 지으면서 가까운 회사에 다니고 있다

우리 딸은 29세 아들은 27세 모두 직장에
다니고 있단다 애들 엄마도 직장에 다니고 있고

30년만에 쓰는 글이라 배울라체가 앞뒤가
안맞지만 이해하고 들어주렴

정말 미안하다 지영아 아들 용서해다

이소현 선생님
만약에 편지가 오면 이곳으로 보내주세요

전북 정읍시 하모동 865번지
　　　　(주) 대광

우편번호 580-020

I. FIELD

In the X Pastoral

Yes, there is a field, in the middle, a tree sways
       full with greenness, edible chartreuse.
Yes, there is a rusted red tractor roving
       up & down tugging the bailing machine, dropping
square bales of hay, scattered forgotten furniture dotting
       the view of the horizon. No rain-cloud, no shiver,
no loneliness, just the sun's gold saturation, & the girl
       in her bird-red coat, bending over, cupping
hands together, making train-whistles vibrate through blades of grass.
       At yard sales, she'll learn to look for tall glasses, for lemonade
& iced tea, & long-handled silver spoons, long enough
       to stir in the sugar for the men working the fields, stacking
the hay bales high on the tractor's flatbed. Inside the farmhouse, white
       paint peeling, her grandma rolls out secrets
from the flour drawer, making biscuits, donuts, telling the little girl
       she belongs, belongs, belongs in that field of hay & corn,
not in the field, far away, where women bend, pluck & place
       their harvest in baskets. Hands over hands, overpouring.

1

Crown of Yellow

The colors of the fields flush with goldenrod.

Butter browned in a pan for the sauce to dress a dead fish.

Yellow yolks make cake, custards, or the exact shade for stasis.

Or shame. Yellow, I think, is always this way.

A primary color, it arrived in packages of crushed natural iron oxide from a quarry in France.

Combine yellow with red, make orange. Shades shift by proportion.

The painter tells me about his color palette choices, not the grey fear-sphere spinning in my mind, or anything I know something about.

The beehive above swings out; yellow bits flit here & there.

How yellow the yellow finches' bodies, how they lift so easily into the air.

It is the in-between color—traffic lights say, *Pause.*

The striking of a single ray of sunlight can cause cancerous cells to grow, mutate.

Paint the kitchen walls a shade of yellow—warms & comforts.

Color of the piss puddle I left on the hardwood floor. Little ballerina shoes tiptoed around the mess. I did raise my hand / I did ask to go / I did try to do the right thing.

Tutus & twirls. Mrs. Stein said, *Wait. Hold it!* Her black leotard stretched over the curvature of her small breasts rising with her commands.

If you prefer gold fillings & can afford them, the dentist will fill your teeth.
Gold is a soft metal.

Combine yellow with blue, make green.

Are we back in the field, yet? Why do I ever leave? The forest needs no grammar.
Water splits rock. Hawk shreds yellow birds' feathers.

The mind, an unending sieve.

Dandelion wine is made from the tufts of yellow heads collected & boiled.
Alcohol is made for adults. Some bitterroot.

Never dress Asian babies in yellow, my mother instructs me. *Clashes with their skin.*
I learned from you, she says.

& there is a fox running the median line on the bumpy road & I'm driving fast, headlights off, because
there is a full-bodied yellow moon & I want to move in the dark like I know exactly, no precisely,
without any hesitation, where I am going, barreling ahead.

Each hour the light changes, each minute angles shift.

Skylights are key in the studio: naked. Put on my skin in yellow layers—how many?
Painter, show me what you see.

I prefer to sleep through sunrise. I trust the heliocentric turning of things that are difficult
to understand.

About yellowface I cannot say enough.

What is enough?

The channeling knife is the tool to carve a lemon twist. I use it. Hover over the glass,
make the cut, infuse the air in the space above the liquid with the essence of the fruit.

Once, I plucked an entire bucket of lemons & lavender. Made lemonade.

I don't believe in that phrase…because my mother took to the tug of the bottle.
Vomit is often yellow.

In another dream, I am the lone sunflower, in the field, shaken by the anticipation
from the smell of the oncoming distant rain.

Greenhousing

I'll push against—
        what did you say—any
                edge. An orchid cannot
impregnate it-
        self. Stamen & pistil
strike as dirty words, but are necessary.
        I know how
                to push
        against the glass. As the variable, X,
I was a sticky mess made from two bodies
        colliding, the way swells rise
& fall counting beats per second. Did she want
        him? Did he
want her? Where did
      he put
his hands
        when he made me?
(X knows X can't ask such questions). X knows
father tried to keep X
after she died, but then he put
        her somewhere else
                where he thought
he could remember
where he left her.
        Gloved hands. Dirty mouth.
Greenery & potted
        plants with roots & beginnings,
                all must grow downward
        first before
            they burst.

Case Number: K83-5XX

[blonde hair, blue eyes *is beauty*]

noted: baby coos, laughs

[all mirrors, she'll think, are liars]

noted: no more tremor-like movement

[slanted eyes, round face, monolids]

noted: *adoptable* stamped on documents
tucked away in folders in file cabinets

[*X*, for *adoptable* = loveable]

diagnosis, linguistic: _____

[shhhhhh, shush now]

Primary Color

X shouldn't go bare-chested in the garden
X takes it off anyway Girl nipples Sun-seeped
lemonade Why does it matter Rows Muddied
ankles & feet Unfolded map
  Yes-of-course-don't-be-silly leave-it-off
her father declares not time
for shame Yet It takes three years to grow
asparagus More for apples Rely on bees
pollen dust her bare backside Compost Bucket of feed
paint in oily streaks the pears & blocks Egg shells
the body can be rendered *X*'ll learn later
from the boy who asks to hang her figure
on a gallery wall Skin unscented not metallic
the fresh red-stain blooms afterwards
on the white carpet

On Creating False Memory

late blooming goldenrod shudders in the uncut field
       & all rests fallow until next year's upward swing
so let the smoky wood-burn smell that won't leave your clothes
       linger from the bonfire the night before the laundry basket
still not full enough the smell wafts & makes you feel the rub
       of shoulders meeting in straight-backed wooden chairs
not-so-silent skin on skin while the pulsing dark quickens & crickets thrum
       their strident chords no real harmony & you felt winded
from two flights of stairs & remember sinking into a lake holding
       up your entire body its own lake-river-pool-bathtub
a trace of you inside an unnamed uterus & everything you can't recall
       take it all back & the dreams blur out of focus & reach towards
past lives you can't hold & the horses ran away & came back
       to the fields to gorge themselves off freshly dropped apples
& the moon was a sudden quicksilver than full & rising & rising
       & there's nowhere to go but touch the bulge of amethyst a bird's egg
a notion of what's solid the stone not the filaments that you manage to warp
       & weave through un-fulfilled hearts like cornhusk silk
threaded through holes in the sieve

Swarm

I left him standing there by a decaying log, mouth
agape, no sound, still & shocked by the swarm

of angry wasps propelling themselves out of the nest we'd hit
with our bikes under the spruce on the east end of the property.

It was a sun that slanted long & low at the edge of
the pines; it was a soft breeze lifting the scent of grass

just mowed, drying in the distant field, waiting
to be bound, made into rectangles, stacked. What can I do

but pedal away faster? I don't look back. Not once. *You've
gotta make hay when the sun shines*, say the old-timers. I make

the hay sway. I make the wasps retreat back to their nest.
Or I make him cry & wail: rock beats scissors / scissors

beats paper / paper beats rock / I let wasps beat up my little
brother because I don't pull him away, I don't yell, *Pick up*

your bike. Run! My lungs load with panic. No release.
Because I don't take his chubby hands, run with him towards

the house to the stone steps, don't implore him to save
himself. I see his face: still puffy. Wasps sting again & again.

They're the ones who won't die after just one stabbing.
So, they tickle him, they caress his skin, they stroke

him like soft gusts lift leaves, makes shadows play on the lemonade
glasses set out for the men coming in from haying in the hot fields.

Each glass glistens, the ice dissolving back into its original form.
Liquid pooling on the glass tabletop. It's true. The wasps

found their way down his shirt. Later, we have to paint
his back pink to cover up the redness, the blotchy

raised welts. Later, we have to go back to get his bike,
resting where he flung it on its side. Pedals still.

Letter to the Woman on the Plane

You, who transported *X* number of small
squirming packages from one country to another,
of course, only remember *me*. I was delightful.
I did not holler the whole way on that long flight.
I let you sleep; although, refused the bottle.
Maybe you thought your job was holy, newly anointing
another white mother; or was it just another job,
delivering bundles made from panting & groping
around in the dark? Dried up semen, tangled bed sheets.
All those mothers waiting in all those terminals, outstretched
arms, fingers extended, as you handed over baby after baby
to home after home, practicing how to re-create *family*.
Why, even now, do I practice this insistence on beauty?

여 8개월
birth- 2.6 = 4.40 lbs
Oct 5 - 3.4 kg. 7.48 lbs
wt 8m ~ 2.2

Average Measurements for Korean Children

나이 (Age)	Weight	Height	Head	가슴
New Born	3.34	51.1	34.7	333.6
1 month	5.21	57.4	38.3	38.9
2~				
3~				
4~				
5~				
6~	8			
7~	8			
8~	8			
9~	8.17	71.5	44.5	45.4
10~	9.			
11~	9.33	75.3	45.3	45.6
12~	9.58	75.8	45.7	46.4
15~	10.11	78.5	46.4	47.3
18~	10.55	80.4	47.0	48.2
19~	10.80	82.4	47.2	
2 Year~	11.84	85.5	47.6	
2½~	12.55	88.5	48.2	

Head	Chest
34.4	33.6
38.0	38.3
39.2	40.3
40.1	41.1
40.9	41.9
41.5	42.4
42.3	42.8
43.0	43.5
43.2	43.9

나이 (Age)	Weight	Height					Chest
3 Year~	13.25	91.9					
3½~	13.91	94.1					
4~	14.85	97.9					
4½~	15.68	101.5			53.0		64.1
5~	16.71	105.0			53.6	76.4	66.2
5½~	17.67	107.7					69.1
6~	18.49	110.6					
6½~	18.86	112					
7~	20.6	117.					
8~	22.69						

105.6	49.5	49.2	53.4	72.1
109.2	54.0	53.3	52.7	69.1
112.1	54.9			
105.9	56.3	50.0	51.7	58.0
154.0	53.7		52.2	59.8
			52.7	61.9

Origins & Forms: Eight Sijos

1

Math is mostly equations: 1 plus 1, 2 plus 2, plus...
also formulas, so many designed variables—
to keep someone alive calculate, add & subtract the costs.

2

What if hands pull down stars, guide them inside a round belly?
What if this is how a spirit dives, twists into a body?
What is built up from bones: Fingernails. Skin. Flesh animated.

3

Grandmother's fingers tightened around her bundled form,
(a thing) spitting, begging, for warmth from her hunched over
indecisive back—she knew the math would not compute.

4

This is where I'll learn how to cast the rod to find the fish,
or skim the water to chase Jesus bugs, walking on the surface
by some trick of tension & balanced perfection. Keep count.

5

What does this form do that others don't? I'll force the issue
of Korean poetic form, composing these sijos. In this way,
I'll be closer to her genetics, her bloodlines—strands fraying.

6

This is where I learn how to skip stones across how many
lakes? Making circles, again, hearing the sound of stone on water.
Oars cut cleanly through its flat surface—stars, so many stars.

7

In the heat, grandmother fans her face, puts bottle to lips,
flicks flies off her head, & tries to conjure up a dead mother's
face, show her a smile she'll never remember, nor this thick night.

8

Always those hands keep plucking stars from the heavens, make
constellations inside bodies, make more mothers. I see how form
& origins are stories—I am all those mathematical distances.

While in Miryang, Searching

Stand on the street & look down it:
all the houses balloon inside with strangers
going about their daily tasks, boiling
water for tea, for baths, for rice.

Stopping in Miryang is the guide's idea;
he thinks it is the most probable place
from where her ancestors originate.

Headline: "South Korea Hospital Fire
Kills at Least 37 People"

It's the fourth hit for "Miryang"
on Google search results.

Hunger. Park in front of the noodle shop.
Piping hot bowls, opaque liquid so thick
spoons dip in & dredge up savory treasures
under the floating seaweed. *X*'ll stuff
herself on this dish, perhaps made by
some distant relative.

The fire licked concrete walls,
peppered the streets with ash, shards
of glass. *X* learns it was in winter,
in the night.

What burns, burns.

The waitress squats
feet flattened & planted in full
on the floor, a flexibility
lost on *X* as she shifts in her seat.
Tight American muscles—tautness
that will not bend & elongate.

The women of Miryang climb
to the summits of their foothills, walking
to protest construction of
large electric power lines planned
to run through sacred burial sites.

They have to answer
to their ancestors in the next life.

Yes, it is true
noodle dishes are delicious.

Was the fire around the corner?
Down the street? Can we drive there, now?

X reaches out—tries grasping,
coils tips of fingers around
her ancestors' thin visages.

Each shimmers.

An ash-cloud floats away.

Still Life with Watermelon Seeds, Mannequin, Dead Mouse

Serrated edge flash shards of light on white walls, carving
up the watermelon slices that drip juice down our thin
brown arms, my father salts his pink slice-smiles, tiny
grains melt in. A neon sign, in my mouth, this shock of fruit-flesh.

Don't swallow the seeds! he warns & I want to so bad & I'm bad.
Under the covers, eyes shut, I see twisted vines tumble, roots
embed in my stomach's black, new green shoots slide
over my pink tongue, thick...We spit out the slippery seeds

onto the stone patio. The summer night air quivers & the gash
on her left knee pulses. Watch third person shift focus: so
barely scabbed over, she'll dig up poems from dirt, she'll run
all those races, she's not split, not the furry body opened

on its side, tail limp, she's not the mouse's intestine peeping out,
she's not the one that glistens. The cat's claw, the hawk's talon.
What flourishes withers in the heat. In the photograph, all seated
in a row, on the front porch of the log cabin, bodies pixelated,

the mannequin next to her, I mean next to *me*, is some joke
no one gets. A plastic copy of another body—a jab, perhaps,
at my mother. Blonde wig & lush lashes propped up
next to father on the stoop. Right there. We know what comes

next from practice: drag the coiled green hose from the side of
the house to wash away the seeds.

[translation/1]

I don't know where to start. Now that I sit down to right, my hands are trembling, I am nervous and I am also little bit worried. I always wanted to see you. I always thought about you during 30 years. I know that a parent who abandoned baby has nothing to say, but I always thought about you, wanted to see you and was curious about you. I gave you up for adoption because your mother passed away after a month you were born. She left you like that. A first I decided to raise you with my mother but I am a farmer and I had no time to nurture you and our situation was not well enough. I finally decided to send you away and called the institution to let you meet a nice parent rather than me. So please forgive me. After 30 years, now I want to know if you had met nice parents, if you have grown up well, if you are married since you are 30 years old now. Please forgive me who could not support you well. I am sorry.

Few month later after sending you away, I met a woman and got married. We gave birth to two children and raised them since then. I worked at a factory but I left my hometown soon, and now I am living in a small apartment in jeong-up city, Jeollabuk-do.

10 years before I bought a small land in a near small town. I work at a small company and simultaneously doing farm work. My daughter is now 29 years old, and my son is now 27 years-old. Each of them works at a different company. Their mother also has a job. Since it is the first letter I am writing in a 30 years, please understand that the content is not fluently related.

I am sorry, please forgive me ji-young.

17

II. DRESS

Confessional

To build
an ancestral palace

To no longer live
inside the silence
of myself

To rupture like an egg
on lime linoleum

I was sent into the chicken coop
to feed them eggshells

One body feeds another

I am not enough of *X*

It looks like & feels like rain
& the flatness of that grey sky

Is what you think I am
the odious dot of a period
on its arrival.

On Not Fitting In

1

Tiny orange globules of roe, slimy pickled ginger lag behind on my plate. The water in the bubbler gurgles. I slide chopsticks together. Over & over. Chafing enough causes splintering.

2

Cold, so there is wood turning to ash in the stove. It is supposed to be spring, but the ground is all leaf litter & damp & streams swollen from snow melt. Thick ice thrusts itself up; it pummels the shoreline of the lake, plucks up docks, beaching them.

3

Rice misses my mouth. I forget the reason why I'm hungry. The spoon walks off the table taking miso with it. Yellow cake or softening lemons or custard in cups lifted to lips with silver spoons.

4

Ice will melt on its own. It needs no assistance. Some butterfly, when given a chance, will drink blood. Rubbing two sticks together makes fire. Facts are things to hold on to.

5

He says he's fine. We are driving to nowhere. It is a place. We *are* fine. His dog—not mine—naps in the backseat. Body: a half-moon.

6

A shimmering splinter of particles, a dead star's light rays, are what reach our heavy lidded, slit eyes. It shoots across the sky. What is peripheral?

7

From the shower drain I pull strands, matted together, of my own dark hair. I push the vacuum around the room; the circles puff up dust, dead skin cells, lint.

8

No, he says, I think they are almond trees. White cotton ball flowers hanging onto thin scraggly branches. 50 gallons of water for one almond.

9

One slit. One eye. It's mine. Soft-core yellow, cold ash.

It Was a Yellow Light

Early mornings, I waited for the school bus, tiny hands clasping
thin backpack straps, lunch inside a crinkled brown paper bag, tacky

white fluff & peanut butter stuck to the cheap Ziploc. The bus arrived
at 7:05 a.m. The yellow morning light was a warm puddle—soft, I could

touch it. On the braided carpet, the dog's fur poked through. At 7:01 a.m.,
a miniscule wave would ripple in the floorboards, the grainy wood

shifting & then I dropped into myself. A vortex. Swirling. My mouth
flapping open, swallowing air, wanting safety from the yellow orb moving up

through my feet. 7:02 a.m. The dog barks. I want to grab his tail, pull
on it—I think: *I am here*. Hold on to the doorknob. Don't turn it. A sucking

sound like cupping a seashell to the ear & roiling ocean hits my eardrums.
The carpet wobbles & spins, faster & faster. The furniture grows legs

& starts to walk towards me; the television a brilliant red light, flashing
like a disco ball swinging or the iridescent scales of a caught fish; the lamps

flicker & I am the center of my own vortex, trudging cinderblock
legs through water, every water. I swear it. I try to tread

above the clock's secondhand poised to tick each millimeter. 7:03 a.m.
Two more minutes until the bus arrives. Two more minutes until getting on.

Two more minutes until I am born. Yes, I was the cell dividing, touching the shore,
turning into foam floating out towards the moon's rippling reflection. No.

I was the roar of all that liquid filling a woman's womb. No, I wasn't there yet.
Not inside. I was the breeze brushing against her cheek in the lush golden field.

Grass swaying. Until two minutes. Bees, in my mouth, muffling the sound, no,
the song I was trying to sing. The clock's secondhand advanced, gears turned.

Everything shifts until each molecule finds its place. 7:05 a.m. The carpet slides
over the wide chasm. There is no water left. I board the bus.

Lament for Some Other Saigon

My father taught me
feet are something
to care for, cradle.
He won't talk
about his time
in 'Nam. I remind
people his age
too much of hot,
sticky green foliage
flapping in their faces,
or steam rising up
from rice paddies
the platoons waded
through all morning,
crossing in the open,
barrels loaded, sighted,
ready for a fight.
Yellow. Roses.
That is what they
sent home to their wives
to shrivel in glass vases.
My face, a big yellow
moon, rises in their
nightmares, my face
a howling monkey,
a ripe watermelon rind
grinning back at them.
Or perhaps it's my hair
that troubles them:
black braid bouncing
with the rocking
movements
of the swing.
Whose hand
sears its own shape
on my skin?

My skin will turn
to crisp brown
under any sun.
My eyes will holster
any loaded rifle.
My father is an ant
moving through tall
grass, boots filling
with mud & muck.
He never talks about
anything else.
He's the slap of the wind
hitting my face.
His yellow balloon
silence is what fills
the room, but I'm the air
taking up the space
between his ribcage.
A face like mine
walks among others
in his dreams.

Letter To My Adoptee Diaspora

Deep scars on their backs, most manatees float
too close to the top. It is their nature, wired
for a specific solitary frequency. Up to 1,200 lbs.
they spend most of their days hovering
near the watery surface air & grazing.
Headline: "Korean orphans languish in system
as tradition, new laws make adoption difficult."
We are the sea cows afloat, munching on vats
of kimchi, shoveling ramen into our mouths,
trying to make us "Real Asians." They say
manatees replace their teeth throughout their lives.
What do we replace for DNA—a house, new cars,
inadequate lovers—while propellers split open
our ballooned backs? Do you feel like you
were robbed of your culture?
Often, awake in the night, in bed, I think of us.
So many. Just floating. I wonder if you long
for an unnamed touch or smell, a sense of gnawing
from the inside & if you cannot reach the surface,
then you, dear adoptee, are not alone.
I am lonely, too.

Broken Palette :: a retrospective in panels

There is a Korean saying that a person is born behind a screen and dies behind a screen. In the past, when it was common for babies to be born at home, a folding screen, called byeongpung (lit. "wind blocker") in Korean, would be used to turn a space into a delivery room.

1.

Late afternoon, on the streets of Seoul, nerves misfire,
your tongue taps soundless against rows of stiff teeth.

At the entrance to the rail station, a woman who looks like you
approaches for directions & then yellow-bellied & afraid,

all you can do is shake your head, hand cupped to your ear,
& pantomime you're deaf / dumb / don't understand

& this is when you know how a black hole swallows.

2.

Swallowing toxic tea, 1,000 years ago, made flesh immune to maggots.
A CT scan shows the mummified body seated in its own preservation;
each sip was a choice. How to explain the hummingbird's darting

split tongue? Cows bend to the saltlicks in the field. Birds,
with their ability to fly, are still governed by gravity & daughters
by their mothers' habits. Zebras, especially the young, rely on pattern

recognition, stripes identify to whom each belongs. Scientists track
whales by their flukes dipping in & out of vast seas, while on land,
slugs have four noses & the heart of a shrimp is located in its head.

The koala's fingerprints mimic a human's so well they can confuse
crime scene specialists. So, another mammal must have left her imprint,
a light tenderness on your neck—how else do you expect one mother

to stand in for another? During mating, the female mallard's head
is held under water. Almost drowning is touching creation.

3.

Yellow, the level of attachment you're capable of. *Over the course of centuries, color was first defined as matter, then as light, & later as a sensation: that of light falling on an object received by the eye, & transmitted to the brain.*

~

Your college boyfriend: "You're a Twinkie. You know, yellow on the outside, white on the inside."

4.

We harvest the bark in late fall from the mulberry trees
stiff in rows in the back field. The mature ones, hardy,
weathered & taut, produce enough to carry us. Pulp-making

takes the time it takes. Often too long. Consider the costs of
hanji for our dividing screens. Pound the bark on stone
over & over with a wooden baton. Long fibers relent. The mash

is cooked, boiled, continuously stirred. Laid on the heat drier,
brushed & ready to hang, bark becomes paper. What about process
makes this matter? To you, to anyone? In a dream, the white

sheets are fluttering, the wind now visible. Only in lucidness
do you arrive at knowing the shape of your eyes, the angle
of your nose, the cadence of unspoken longing.

5.

Driving dirt roads, paint peels & flakes off dilapidated
clapboards—the sky a bowl of lemons. Hours spent in the sun
deepens the skin. "Asians don't raisin," remarks a friend.
With a slap you apply sunscreen anyway.

~

Because the Mary Kay in-home beauty consultant, opening
& closing the sleek compacts of blush & eye shadow, pulls out
her foundation chart & notes the differences between your color
palette & your mother's, you never learn to wear makeup.

In the 90's infomercial, the cosmetic designer shares her eureka
moment: adding splashes of milk to coffee mimics
the foundation shades she'll mix to match skin tones.

~

During your year-as-a-barista, you learn to make a latte so hot
it burns the hand through the cup's sleeve. It's the way
the well-heeled woman with the Kate Spade bag wants it.

6.

dear mother,

[   ]   unbearable

        yellowbird [   ]

hot water   tea   bowl
cut or sewn   break

rest   [   ] sleep

[   ]

~~I told you~~   there's a whole country,

a landscape painting inside me—

[   ]

~~I know~~ you meant to [   ]

7.

While the painter mixes yellow with blue, the gardener curates
a living palette & starts sunflowers inside, an oscillating fan

strengthens their stalks. In the 17th century, at the height
of the Dutch tulip trade, painters mixed innumerous shades

of yellow. In France, caves are now closed off to visitors;
a simple puff of breath accelerates the painted colors' fade.

Nothing lasts. This color study is not possible without
negative space, or history & yet it seems false to render

lives as plants or color. We do it anyway: cadmium-lemon-
honey-flaxen-canary-banana-butter-mustard-blonde...

while the bees tuck inside swelling buttercups, their legs laden
with pollen retracing lines on an invisible map. At least the deer,

leaping away from danger, don't appear to be lonely. Stifled
by this rural description, you see only what fills the foreground,

but when you step back into the field, at dusk, your ancestors' faces
golden, wave a fading welcome, & then you believe in the dream

& the field you imagine merges to become the field you step into.

On Meeting My Biological Father

Mostly, I don't think about him at all
as I go about my day, hanging laundry to dry,
brushing teeth, making tea, & somehow,
he never appears in dreams, & perhaps,
I do feel a bit guilty about the lack
of his presence, how it doesn't take up
space in my subconscious, & then I need
to remind myself that it happened at all,
that afterward, at a pork hibachi restaurant,
on some street I cannot name, in Korea, a server
frets over the meat, uses scissors to cut up
strips, flipping them as the juices sizzle & slip
down onto the coals in front of us. My father teaches
me to use chopsticks, how to fold the hot pork strips
in lettuce, add sliced green onions,
freshly pressed tofu, radishes.
With this stranger I've just met, I sit
on the floor, share this meal. Gestures,
a smile here & there, is what I can say.
I don't remember the quality of the light
only that he said he didn't take
my mother to the hospital—it was
because of family debt, a cloud
hanging over him—so she died
& he was left with me—small &
screeching, with no milk, no bottle,
formula so expensive. What to do?
When did he realize he couldn't care?
Again, I try to remember what
it was like in the orphanage,
in a country where I've never lived,
in a foreign tongue. He holds
my hand, strokes the back of it, says,
how good it is to see I am grown,
I even resemble my mother, says he's
happy, asks if I'm happy, too.

Korea Doll Box

Chatting away about how much they love, are obsessed with, Asian cultures, two cashiers in the local grocery: *How can you tell the difference between them; they're all the same! Chinese or Japanese? Same thing.* Ooo, how much they adore them. The woman bagging my groceries: *I'm going to get my DNA tested. Who knows, I might be Korean!* The checkout woman hands me the change. Her chubby fingers, be-decked with gaudy gold rings. Her jaw moves up & down, lip-smacking her chewing gum loudly. I take my face out the door; carry heavy bags, eggs nestled on top. The change clinks in my pockets & stones lodge in my throat.

> she's encased in glass
> pearls & strands of hair woven
> greenfields goldenrod

adoptable = loveable = adoptable = loveable = adoptable = loveable = adoptable = loveable =
adoptable = loveable = adoptable = loveable = adoptable = loveable = adoptable = loveable =
adoptable = **loveable** = adoptable = loveable = **adopt**able = loveable = adoptable = loveable =
adoptable = loveable = adoptable = loveable = adoptable = loveable = adoptable = loveable =
adoptable = loveable = adoptable = loveable = adoptable = loveable = adoptable = loveable =
adoptable = loveable = adoptable = loveable = adoptable = loveable = adoptable = loveable =
adoptable = loveable = adoptable = loveable = adoptable = loveable = adoptable = loveable =
adoptable = loveable = adoptable = loveable = adoptable = loveable = **adopt**able = loveable =
adoptable = **love**able = adoptable = love**able** = adoptable = loveable = adoptable = loveable =
adoptable = loveable = adoptable = loveable = adoptable = loveable = adoptable = loveable =
adoptable = loveable = adoptable = loveable = adoptable = loveable = adoptable = loveable =
adoptable = loveable = adoptable = loveable = adoptable = loveable = adoptable = **loveable** =

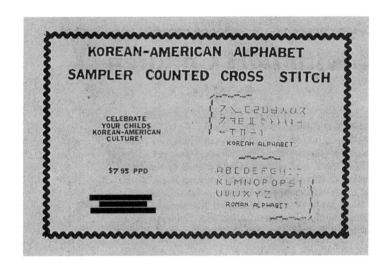

adoptable = loveable = adoptable = loveable = adoptable = loveable = adoptable = loveable =
adoptable = loveable = adoptable = loveable = adoptable = loveable = adoptable = loveable =
adoptable = **loveable** = adoptable = loveable = **adopt**able = loveable = adoptable = loveable =
adoptable = loveable = adoptable = loveable = adoptable = loveable = adoptable = loveable =
adoptable = loveable = adoptable = loveable = adoptable = loveable = adoptable = loveable =
adoptable = loveable = adoptable = loveable = adoptable = loveable = adoptable = loveable =
adoptable = loveable = adoptable = loveable = adoptable = loveable = adoptable = loveable =
adoptable = loveable = adoptable = loveable = adoptable = loveable = **adopt**able = loveable =
adoptable = **love**able = adoptable = love**able** = adoptable = loveable = adoptable = loveable =
adoptable = loveable = adoptable = loveable = adoptable = loveable = adoptable = loveable =
adoptable = loveable = adoptable = loveable = adoptable = loveable = adoptable = loveable =
adoptable = loveable = adoptable = loveable = adoptable = loveable = adoptable = **loveable** =

35

Dear Connie Chung

Marooned on islands, *X* are hemmed in
by the rise & fall of white frothing sea foam,
but you were boon & burden, a glowing moonface
beamed into our living rooms.

Reliable visits occasioned consistent moments
of glee. As a castaway, to survive, *X* endured
lack of unicorns, whole milk & we made claims to
sustenance of hot dogs with mustard, waking grief,
mac & cheese.

Framed in the square black TV box, you gestured,
well-coiffed, from a fixed point at your desk, reporting
on world news in a French blue blazer. *X* learned
to decipher code from your features, like ours.
Shooting off smoke signals & flares, useless.

Beauty Being Beauty

We flipped through the magazine
& didn't recognize her transformed
in the glossy spread, lighting just right,
hair shiny black, cheekbones round, dark eyes lustrous.
Lucky. Selected for Asian Beauty & I wanted to be her,
chosen off the streets of New York for *Vogue*.
Yes, vanity, but what if I am always five, always
running from the coach's son who's hollering
"Flat face!" & I'm always questioning, don't
recognize my own fingers tracing my nose (not flat)
in mirrors, the contours of a face reflected back in 2-D.
Coveted forms: bound tulip-sized feet, docile or timid,
thin yet unbreakable—of course, of course.
Let's line up all the fetishes
in rows like hardened pearls.

Continuum

On its leash, the womb I walk around conforms
to the size & shape its contents require & the idea

of a glass vase nesting purple-bruised irises rises in my mind.
Daily, storage increases along the tiny folds of brain matter.

Right now someone is memorizing the sequence for *pi*,
thousands of digits, but how to solve for *X*? Babies' attachments

to their mothers, writes experts, is a continuum of bonding—
It's happening everywhere! Proof theorems, calculate imaginary

numbers, test equations that break with tiny teeth marks. Bites.
Aliens mutate & swell inside their hosts. Comfort them.

Find abandoned clear plastic bins on wheels on hospital wards,
soft pink & blue blankets mimic absent arms. Surprise

yourself with your own limits, but why bother, if *X* is not
possible to define without context? The librarian explains

how her collection expands & contracts by the banned book
enthusiast who hides dangerous volumes out of order, props up

the Bible. I am a modern woman. I choose my extent. Fatty
deposits. Cellulite. Armpit hair. Practice a daily regimen

of strict joy metered out in white oval pills. Ecosystems
vary due to stresses on their systems—it's never enough just to love.

Field Dress Portal

~ Lauren Woods, Field Dress, 7' x 6', oil on linen

a yellow orb shifts against the shock of dark vertical bark, her back
       split diagonal, flayed & a bright fleshy
suspension in the copse of trees, her hooves scrape packed dirt, legs
       sway like she's dancing on hindquarters & I could
take her body inside me, like the medicine I need, or wrap her
       skinned hide, congealed blood flaking, a cloak against the coming
night & I'd wear her ears, pin her white-warning-tail to my backside
       as regalia for all the deer-dead, but the painting only approaches
her in 2-D—a portal of slim brushstrokes, paint upon paint, so I step
       into the field, from the left, outside the frame, push through tall
burnished grasses, bending slightly, my feet crush crickets, trample
       late blooming goldenrod & I let the heat of the day leak out
of the air like a balloon popped & swirling, so I can become Field. Dress. Portal.
       What is the *worst* possible thing to ask of yourself? Maybe believing
in whatever makes demands on your own inner life, like how love
       is supposed to save even the most hardened ones. Only this dead doe's
head bows & whistles to the others, come find me—quick, like light,
       or like all the seedpods' sudden dispersal, their unrealized progeny float
away without a care for the end result.

[translation/2]

I don't know where to start. Now that I sit down to right, my hands are trembling. I am nervous and I am also little bit worried. I always wanted to see you. I always thought about you during 30 years. I know that a parent who abandoned baby has nothing to say, but I always thought about you, wanted to see you and was curious about you. I gave you up for adoption because your mother passed away after a month you were born. She left you like that. A first I decided to raise you with my mother but I am a farmer and I had no time to nurture you and our situation was not well enough. I finally decided to send you away and called the institution to let you meet a nice parent rather than me. So please forgive me. After 30 years, now I want to know if you had met nice parents, if you have grown up well, if you are married since you are 30 years old now. Please forgive me who could not support you well. I am sorry.

Few month later after sending you away, I met a woman and got married. We gave birth to two children and raised them since then. I worked at a factory but I left my hometown soon, and now I am living in a small apartment in jeong-up city, Jeollabuk-do.

10 years before I bought a small land in a near small town. I work at a small company and simultaneously doing farm work. My daughter is now 29 years old, and my son is now 27years-old. Each of them works at a different company. Their mother also has a job. Since it is the first letter I am writing in a 30 years, please understand that the content is not fluently related.

I am sorry; please forgive me ji-young.

40

III. PORTAL

Six Persimmons

after Muqi Fachang

The fruit is all bold brushstrokes
& negative space in an organized line.
There's one askew; absent color haunts
their shape. Faded orbs. Flat, but plump.
In stalls, she'll find dried ones, packaged;
the heft of each surprises. Winter lasts
longer than one wants. What is omitted
in those thick art history books—
place them in bowls of rice, to keep
from bruising.

Anti-Pastoral

In the fields, they were pecking;
X shot the crows, bodies slack,
In the dirt, their wings settle.
X strung 'em up to warn the others.

X shot the crows, bodies slack,
To protect the crops, yes,
X strung 'em up to warn the others;
Birds, too, have memory. I do nothing—

Roll corncobs in butter, pass the salt.
My defenses strangled—yes?
About the tattooed crow, I say nothing.
Birds, too, have memory. I do nothing—

X protects the crops because, yes,
Nothing about hunger is passive.
Birds, too, have memory. I do nothing—
Goldenrod bends in the breeze.

Nothing about hunger is passive.
In the fields, they were pecking;
Goldenrod bends only in the breeze.
In the dirt, the wings settle.

Initial Gestures

Sitting in a circle
at the baby shower, I think
about the pressure
it takes to push small
square teeth through skin.

You just don't spend enough time
around them.

A friend tending
to her newborn, texts me pics
of the scrunched face, tells me
she already loves
without condition.

You just haven't met
the right guy.

Men are in the rooms now
cutting the umbilical cords.

Forceps. Backless gowns.
Stirrups. Cold tools.

We're chatting
in circular about
the essentials...
predictable things,
admitting to
an abortion. I was
30 or 31. Whatever.
It doesn't matter.

Stiff movements
make shapes.

In the studio
the painter tells me
about the blank canvas:
one must begin
somehow just as
he assumes
a writer does.

But I could delete
that previous admission
if I wanted to.

I could say
my initial gesture
in this world was
ending
my mother's life;
her death
so I could live.

That's lovely,
& beautiful, how she laid down
her life for you.

When consulting a midwife about
probable cause of death, in 1983,
in Korea, at home, I am told it was likely
from infection & that in those days,
women often birthed on tables,
in long rows, without dividing
screens, all at the same time,

pushing, pushing.

You shouldn't think like that.

You don't know
what really happened.

When I started having sex,
my father told me
—Be careful.
You could die,
just like she did.

"Now, where are you from?"

The question is meant to spark conversation. Bald & graying retirees, in for their discount three-course turkey dinners, wonder about the face of the one who is serving them. Gravy on the side & cranberry sauce in ramekins. You like the word *ramekin*. Stacking plates, scraping them. The sound of cutlery plunking into the bus tub. *Cutlery* sounds more refined than *utensil*. "Your English is so good," remarks the lady in the pearls. You understand her perfectly. The lies they think you tell: I am from Vermont / I am from the sea / I grew up here / I am from the stars / I am from Korea / I am not from Korea./ I am, I am, I...i...i...i...

> red sticky fingers
> plunge inside to turn & tug
> *womb* a kind of cave

Adoptee Citizenship Act of 2018

amends the adoptable = loveable = adoptable = loveable = adoptable = loveable = qualifying children adopted

Currently, adopted must adoptable = loveable = adoptable = loveable = adoptable = loveable = adoptable = loveable =

to qualify for

An individual born outside of the United States automatically adoptable = loveable = adoptable = loveable = adoptable = loveable =

the individual adopted by a U.S. citizen before physically present adoptable = loveable = adoptable = loveable = adoptable = loveable =

never acquired adoptable = loveable = adoptable = loveable = adoptable = loveable =

lawfully

meets such criteria, lawfully automatically physically present adoptable = loveable = adoptable = loveable = adoptable = loveable =

issued to such an individual unless:

subjected to a criminal background check, and

adoptable = loveable = adoptable = loveable = adoptable = loveable = coordinated taken regarding

granted to an individual deported for an offense against another person.

We (or in the Blue House)

Invitations were sent to the first of our kind—
        All is behind us. Come home, child.

The painter's commission, for blue-ing
imported goldenrod to match the house's walls,
allows him to rest & eat his fill for months after.

We find the other children lost in the trees. We
are apologies-made-to-us & what we eat glistens
as portions of ourselves proclaim a repetition
of longing. We only knew we were golden

when we knew we could eat the land, lock
ourselves in X. The bees died overwinter
in their stiff boxes. Each moon was a flipped
rabbit in orbit & barcodes on our necks

dissolved, no imprints left. We, strangers,
touch the land with our feet & spook
the deer back home. Those who make
their own light invent the proportions
they desire. We are our own natural
selection.

Planet Nine, a primordial black hole, new research suggests—

Out here, we billow a diaphanous cloud of black cotton candy, digestible & floating. Where did he leave his bones when he left them? A trapdoor leads to Planet Nine & we spin through the solar system. Five years parade by & I don't call / write / pretend / linger on / don't even think about what he's doing—workin' the docks / suckin' on a cigarette / flickin' the hot red tip into a starless sea. Top physicists in their field still bow down to the mysterious, but I know density & mass. I know loss is a kind of closeness—burnt memory, particles whirring, spirals moving towards a vantablack center—99.9% of all light, absorbed. On another planet, rules could be different. We'd calculate with better tools for the job, use more accurate formulas, solve for X. Dear half-brother, you left a seething black hole & only stars, collapsing—now I see how the most exciting research is exploratory in nature: What if you were married, fat & rich? A father, the good life. What if all revelation is incremental?

The Black Cows in the Foreground

it is unknown
where the bones
of your mother
turned to fragments

none in the painting
of the black cows
so where to grieve
her body

no parcel of land
to plant sorrow
in furrowed rows
the black cows graze

contentedly on autumn's
tough grasses
& goldenrod shifts
like brushstrokes

these mammals' bodies
must feel impending storms
inside the large cavities
of their many stomachs

it is correct to fear
the coming loneliness
when your white mother
dies you will be detached

as feathers as you let
them drift down & tangle
in your hair & know
what can be known

inside you carry the cows,
the mountains, the clouds,
all the hillside's questions:

how did she comb her hair;

where are those strands?
did she wash her feet
in a basin: porcelain or clay;
where did she sleep, in a bed

next to him? on pallet
or mattress with springs?
did she eat daily of dust
or particle, or air; would
she wake in the night

from ghost-terrors,
or from thoughts
of you?

The Half-Sister, Unmet

Paint the edges of an imagined life in a foreign tongue,
in a land rich in exotics: silk hanboks, piled-high beaded

pearl hair pieces, tea ceremonies, swallowing odd animal eggs.
Exotic because it's *over there*, inappropriate, of course,

for fetishizing *the other*. (I am performing). Let's say
how inadequate: my fecundity swells up sudden, a heavy

perfume at the apex before the slope to decay. Our heads
nestled on one pillow, we might have whispered to each other

tiny confessions of who we lusted after, even loved. Sisters. Secret
keepers. Probably, we would have hated each other.

Fishheads (or Fuckheads)

Bang! Backdoor slams. Trash hefted into the dumpster. Bang! Kitchen door opens & the waitress twirls heavy trays & serves up the bacon-blue burgers we've ordered with ketchup & a *here-you-go-sweetie*. The chatter of a small-nowhere-near-nothing-town fills the diner, a lulling hum. Battered fries settle in my stomach with their thick grease. Nice to know you'll get what you want, if you order it right. The formica gleams on the diner table. Suck in cheeks, press pursed lips. I pull the photo up on my device & my father glances at the stranger who made me by semen & blood. He looks up & says *You should be eating fishheads* & I say, *What*? & he says, *Fishheads*. & I say, *What*? & he says, *Fishheads. Instead of burgers...* & I say...*Fuckheads*? Fish don't have vocal chords; they make noise by vibrating muscles. Most brands of lipstick contain fish scales. Catfish have over 27,000 taste buds all over their bodies. Humans? 7,000. Starfish are not fish, neither are jellyfish. My jawbone detaches, elongates & lowers with rows of teeth, sharp & white. In front of the waitress, stopping by just to refill the coffee mugs, drop off the check, call me *sweetie* one last time, I swallow my father whole.

Caspian Lake

~ *for A, K, & R*

Look, no stare, at the water's
tracked surface, moondew forms
in the air.

These grey days I want—
no Prince from Narnia,
no Turkish delight.

~

Bright suited bodies
jump in & out, dogs
prowl for scraps, tans
border on burnt, the scent
of sunscreen is coconut
& sour—we watch
others repeat
our own childhoods.

~

Windowpanes divide
the view of the lake
into sections.

How to halve
the world?

~

We leave them ajar,
so the loons' calls carry & echo
at night inside our bedrooms
in the summer cottage.

~

What-if
we popped all the beach balls
at exactly the same time;
pinpricks violent with precision.

The shape of air made visible.

~

*...and lake time isn't
real time*, she says.

The clouds seem to expand, unending.

~

Caspian—the shape of the lake
named for the drying up, distant sea.

~

The engine for the un-focused mind.

~

My dearest friends cannot have a child.

~

Someone else's belly pushes ahead of her, water
rippling out in front. Concentric circles, eventually,
touch the shoreline.

Rotund is a perfect word.

Her roundness arrives in the space, an instant,
before her wherever she goes.

~

They ask me to write a letter in defense
of their future adoption. I am a good friend.
So, I do it.

~

Perhaps it is important
to know
the things one doesn't want?

Make a list.

~

Caspian is dried up.
Salt residue, all
that's left of an entire
sea—lies I might tell.
For sympathy.

~

The body, when retaining
water, will contain blood
low in sodium. My mother's
doctor tells her to limit her
water intake to ¼ cup a day.

Her lungs are crenulated.
Vast seas.

~

Why can't bodies
who want smaller bodies
inside them *have* them?

~

When I let the water take
over for gravity & I float
in the middle of the lake
I am the X
inside a body.

~

This lake is not
a metaphor.
It is a place. I love—

Notes on Garnets

The almandine type is often used as an abrasive.

Fairy tale plot: jewels tumble out of her mouth for every word uttered.

Her mother says, in the garden, she saw a peripheral-ghost-blur, floating & barely perceptible.

Alabanda, the region in ancient Asia Minor where many garnets were harvested.

Her mother claims they appeared in her jewelry box from the ghost-mother,

who left these red cut gems set in gold wire; an inheritance.

Put out your hand. Make any cut to reveal the river red, subcutaneous & seething.

Tiny pressures inside the earth's contours create rarity in color.

She never wears them: stones caged in crinkled tissue in a black velvet box. Shut tight.

Gems are faceted to let light in. Not cutting is dullness, shadow.

Mostly mined for industrial use; rare & flawless.

From inside, what glow emanates—

I think about what the end might be like, resting on velvet & quiet.

[translation/3]

I don't know where to start. Now that I sit down to right, my hands are trembling, I am nervous and I am also little bit worried. I always wanted to see you. I always thought about you during 30 years. I know that a parent who abandoned baby has nothing to say, but I always thought about you, wanted to see you and was curious about you. I gave you up for adoption because your mother passed away after a month you were born. She left you like that. A first I decided to raise you with my mother but I am a farmer and I had no time to nurture you and our situation was not well enough. I finally decided to send you away and called the institution to let you meet a nice parent rather than me. So please forgive me. After 30 years, now I want to know if you had met nice parents, if you have grown up well, if you are married since you are 30 years old now. Please forgive me who could not support you well. I am sorry.

Few month later after sending you away, I met a woman and got married. We gave birth to two children and raised them since then. I worked at a factory but I left my hometown soon, and now I am living in a small apartment in jeong-up city, Jeollabuk-do.

10 years before I bought a small land in a near small town. I work at a small company and simultaneously doing farm work. My daughter is now 29 years old, and my son is now 27 years-old. Each of them works at a different company. Their mother also has a job. Since it is the first letter I am writing in a 30 years, please understand that the content is not fluently related.

I am sorry; please forgive me ji-young.

When My Mother Returns as X

She multiplies herself to be every single
living thing: a cloud of butterflies, six calves

grazing in the field beyond the pines, grass
bending to the wind's steady pressure. She's

a swarm of bees seeking the dust of golden pollen
hidden in the cups of poppies. She is an X

marks the spot where she made me, the hand
that never fed me, imprinting my DNA

a second time. She is a white moon tipped
over, brimming with milk for a body that's

not there. She multiplies herself to be
every form: the breeze lifting the white curtain;

a pink silver-edged cloud expanding; the night
coming on. When my mother returns, she is

the bitter in my mouth I can't dilute; she swells inside;
she's the branch from which birds will never fly.

WAITING

Many of the children whose pictures appeared in our last issue have not been placed. On these pages are the photos of some of those children who need families. If you are interested in any of these children, please contact Vicki Peterson at the IAI office (965-2▓)

▓▓ last issue ▓▓ ▓▓ eight-year-old ▓▓ ▓▓ we ▓▓ learned ▓▓ ▓▓ has a 13 year old sister to be placed ▓▓ ▓▓ living separately, ▓▓ ▓▓ very much like ▓▓ family ▓▓ together.

▓▓ little charmer ▓▓ turning two. ▓▓ development ▓▓ ▓▓ slow, ▓▓ due to poor stimulation ▓▓ physical problems ▓▓ not ▓▓ entirely ruled out. Her name is ▓▓

▓▓ still looking ▓▓ ▓▓ two little brothers, ▓▓ ▓▓ good health ▓▓ normal in every way. Their names ▓▓ ▓▓ and ▓▓

Several ▓▓ inquired ▓▓ ▓▓ in our last issue ▓▓. ▓▓ available, so ▓▓ thought ▓▓ we would run ▓▓ photo again. ▓▓ ▓▓ turned 6 ▓▓ a very nice little boy.

CHILDREN

█████ siblings █████ stay together. ████ middle child
a boy ███████ two ███ girls. ████ are five, three
Two years are ███ developmentally normal
currently in the ███████ Baby Home. Their names
████████ and █████

███ three ███████
██████ foster home
██████ need █ home to-
gether. ████████
████████ 10 years old.
████████ 5 and almost
3 years. ████████
████████████ They
████████ developmentally
normal.

This ███ ███████
some ████ problems but it
████ too early
certain. She is
████ Her name
████████

This sweet little
███████ girl ████ suf-
fered burns,primarily
████████ head.
████ less severe
████ her body
████ require
grafting. ████ needs
loving ████ to help
████████ needs.

████████ baby boy
poor head ████████ an ex-
████ startle reflex. Otherwise,
████ happy, responsive █████
His name is ████████

Notes

The opening two pieces titled "[untranslated]" are images of a handwritten letter from the poet's biological father. Three erasure poems are interrogations of the English translation.

"Waiting Children" repurposes a section (p.10–11) from the Summer 1983 newsletter published by *Wide Horizons*, which was a publication of the formerly named International Adoptions, Inc. This organization still exists today under the name Wide Horizons. Used with permission. Collaged flowers are photos courtesy of the poet. This piece transforms "waiting children" into flowers and interrogates the idea of "shopping" for children vs. shopping for what to plant in the garden. (To the children in this piece: I hope you are safe, happy, and loved.)

The image in "[American] Sampler" was an advertisement in *OURS Magazine*, November-December, 1983, Vol. 16, No. 6. A nonprofit adoptive support group, OURS, Inc., published this periodical bi-monthly. It is currently still in print as the magazine, *Adoptive Families*. Used with permission. This is from the poet's private adoption documents.

The "Moonface Phases" collage uses a document from the poet's private adoption paperwork archive and a childhood photograph of the poet. Handwriting in the margins is by the adoptive mother—a trace of facts and records.

"Broken Palette" sentences in italics are borrowed from and or influenced by the titles, *Yellow: History of a Color* by Michel Pastoureau, translated by Jody Gladding and *Interaction of Color* by Josef Albers. The epigraph is taken from "Byeongpung: The Folding Screens of Korea" by Min Jung, which appeared in *Korean Literature Now*, July 03, 2021.

The last lines in "Crown of Yellow" subconsciously allude to and honor a poem in the collection, *Talismans* by Maudelle Driskell.

The concept of the "anti-pastoral" is attributed to poet, Vievee Francis and appears in her collection *Forest Primeval*.

"We (or in the Blue House)" refers to an event in October 1998 when 29 adoptees were invited to the Blue House in Seoul, South Korea for a formal apology by president, Kim Dae-Jung.

The sijo is a Korean traditional poetic form, which uses three lines with an average of 14 to 16 syllables per line. The sijos in *Hour of the Ox* by Marci Calabretta Cancio-Bello inspired those in this collection.

Holt International Children's Services was founded by Harry and Bertha Holt in 1956. They adopted eight children from South Korea and lobbied the U.S. government to create a pathway for international adoption. Since the initial first eight adoptees, it is difficult to estimate the number of children who have been adopted from South Korea to the U.S.

The Adoptee Citizen Act of 2018 was introduced in the U.S. Senate on March 8, 2018. This bill amends the Immigration and Nationality Act to grant automatic citizenship to all qualifying children adopted by a U.S. citizen parent. This bill continues to be introduced and has yet to be passed.

DNA testing, searching for biological parents, and birthright trips back to countries of origin are common for international adoptees. The adoption industry has revealed falsified documents and stories of parents being lied to. In some cases, mothers were told their children were going to the hospital and would be returned to them at a later date. In 2013, I was able to meet my biological father due to accurate records. This is not the case for many adoptees.

To my fellow, (transracial) adoptees, this book is for you. May we all continue to tell our own stories.

Acknowledgments

With gratitude to the following publications, in which these poems previously appeared, sometimes in earlier forms:

"Still Life with Watermelon Seeds, Mannequin, Dead Mouse" & "Fishheads (or Fuckheads)" – *Defunct Magazine*, Issue 9

"Broken Palette, All Yellow" – *LEON Literary Review*, Issue 10

"On Creating False Memory" – *The Cortland Review*, Issue 86

"Origins & Forms: Eight Sijos" – *Post Road Magazine*, Issue 38

"Hanji" – *The Shanghai Literary Review*, Issue 6

"Field Dress Portal" – *New England Review*, Volume 41, Number 4

"On Meeting My Biological Father" – *Pleiades*, Summer 2020, Volume 40, Issue 2, Korean American Women Poets Folio, edited by E. J. Koh

"To My Adoptee Diaspora" – *They Rise Like A Wave: An Anthology of Asian American Women Poets*

"Beauty Being Beauty" – *SWIMM Every Day*, September 26, 2019

"Swarm" – *Memorious*, Issue 30

"In the Pastoral I Know" & "Anti-Pastoral" – *Malasana*, online imprint of *The Henniker Review*

"Greenhousing" & "Crown of Yellow" – *Tupelo Quarterly*, Issue TQ17

"Letter to the Woman Who Carried Me on the Plane" & "Now, where are *you* from?" – *Scoundrel Time*

"It Was a Yellow Light" – *The Massachusetts Review*, Winter 2018, Asian American Literature Issue

"Lament for Some Other Saigon" – *Four Way Review*, Issue 13, Spring 2018

"When My Mother Returns as *X*" – *Potluck Magazine*, February 2018

With Gratitude

Thank you, Texas Review Press. To J. Bruce Fuller, director of TRP and my dear poet-friend, I am so grateful for your support and our friendship.

This book was supported in part by the Vermont Arts Council and the National Endowment for the Arts with a 2020 Creation Grant that provided support at a crucial time in the development of this book.

The 2022 Emerging Artist Award in Literature from the St. Botolph Club Foundation provided critical support.

The Vermont Studio Center's residency in November 2018 offered invaluable time and space, and deep community. The Rona Jaffe Foundation's generous support was life changing. I am honored to have been a Rona Jaffe Foundation Graduate Fellow in Poetry in the MFA Program for Writers at Warren Wilson College.

The Frost Place, Bread Loaf Environmental Writers' Conference, Banff Centre's Writing Studio, and the Minnesota Northwoods Writers' Conference, are all places where I have found community with fellow writers—thank you.

Thank you to Friends of Writers and the Holden Fund for Diversity.

My deepest gratitude goes to the community at Warren Wilson College's MFA Program for Writers. I am nothing without you all, but especially to the following: Brooks Haxton, Daniel Tobin, C. Dale Young, Christine Kitano, Sally Keith, Debra Allbery, Martha Rhodes, and my July 2016 cohort.

Ellen Bryant Voigt, forever.

Maudelle Driskell, thank you for so much.

The Starlings Collective & my Revisions Writing Group – you keep me going.

Lillian Huang Cummins & Andres Reconco – mi familia of badass writers. All the hearts!!!

I am grateful for the support and friendship of these amazing writers: Tim Karaca, Lane Osborne, Alex McWalters, Eric James Cruz, Joshua Estanislao Lopez, Cindy Sylvester, Hannah Torres Peet, Hieu Minh Nguyen, Cynthia Dewi Oka, Daniel Tam-Claiborne, Maggie Ray, Annick MacAskill, Hannah Dow, Nathan McClain, Jennifer Funk, Kylie Gellatly, Autumn McClintock, Jackie Tilks, Amanda Moore

Thank you to the following: Kathy Chiong & family, Sung Choi & family, Lianna Lee & Geoff Griffiths, Kristina & Ryan Kane & family, C.P. & Carolyn Hsia & family, Anne Weisheipl, Lisa Gilbert Schott, Garrett Werner & family, Katie Ives, Jon & Laura Sykes, Marghie Seymour, Carolyn Kehler (thank you for the author photo!), Moe Garmon, Emily Geiger, Jill Barr, Sarah Wetmore, Sarah Elizabeth Finney, Ms. Smith, Sean Patrick Burke, Mr. & Mrs. Burroughs, Tay Cha, AMC Trails Department (in memoriam, Andrew Norkin), Mary Bouchard & Will Ploof, Hannah Silverstein & Mike Landon, Ben & Sarah Swanson, Chelsea Kendrick & Chad Laflamme, Molly Maloy & Ben Deede, Lily Morgan & Dylan Harry, Rachel & Liz Frierman, Emily Taylor, Kristen Mills, Daniel Zeese, Mara Siegel, Kathy Black, and my colleagues and the Board of Trustees at Vermont Studio Center.

Thank you to Nancy Y. Kim for the use of an image of her piece *how a yellow hollow* as the cover art. I am so grateful to be in collaboration with such a talented and caring artist.

To my family: Gwendolyn Blanche Martin, Ryan Audsley, Douglas & Sandy Audsley, Aunt Bev & Uncle Russell Audsley

To Anna Kehler, Ella, Mila, & Weezer – WOOFS! Love you, always.

To you, dear reader, it has taken my whole life to bring this book into your hands. Thank you for being on the other side.

Xoxo,
Sarah

Author photo courtesy of Carolyn Kehler

SARAH AUDSLEY, a Korean American adoptee raised in rural Vermont, has received support from The Rona Jaffe Foundation, Vermont Studio Center, Banff Centre's Writing Studio, and a Creation Grant from the Vermont Arts Council. Her work appears in *New England Review, The Cortland Review, Four Way Review, The Massachusetts Review, Tupelo Quarterly, Pleiades,* and elsewhere. A graduate of the MFA Program for Writers at Warren Wilson College and a member of The Starlings Collective, she lives and works in Johnson, VT.